Out and About at the Planetarium

By Theresa Jarosz Alberti
Illustrated by Becky Shipe

Special thanks to our advisers for their expertise:

Stephanie L. Parello
Astronomy Education and Events Coordinator
Hayden Planetarium
New York City

Deborah Byrd, Producer and Host,
Earth & Sky Radio Series

Susan Kesselring, M.A., Literacy Educator
Rosemount-Apple Valley-Eagan (Minnesota)
School District

PICTURE WINDOW BOOKS
Minneapolis, Minnesota

The author wishes to thank:

- Dennis Brinkman of the Como Elementary School planetarium in St. Paul, Minnesota;
- Writing pals Tamara, Mary, Terry, Flint, Bob, Trish, and Angela.

Dedicated to my darlings: Bob, Gennie, Leo, and Dante

Managing Editor: Bob Temple
Creative Director: Terri Foley
Editor: Peggy Henrikson
Editorial Adviser: Andrea Cascardi
Copy Editor: Laurie Kahn
Designer: John Moldstad
Page production: Picture Window Books
The illustrations in this book were rendered digitally.

Picture Window Books
5115 Excelsior Boulevard
Suite 232
Minneapolis, MN 55416
1-877-845-8392
www.picturewindowbooks.com

Library of Congress Cataloging-in-Publication Data
Alberti, Theresa Jarosz.
Out and about at the planetarium / by Theresa Jarosz Alberti ;
illustrated by Becky Shipe.
p. cm. — (Field trips)
Summary: Director Solomon gives a guided tour of Star City
Planetarium, where he explains such things as what equipment is used
in a planetarium show and what some of the different objects in the night
sky are. Includes an activity and other learning resources.
Includes bibliographical references and index.
ISBN 1-4048-0299-1 (reinforced lib. bdg.)
1. Planetariums—Juvenile literature. [1. Planetariums. 2. Astronomy.]
I. Shipe, Becky, ill. II. Title. III. Field trips (Picture Window Books)
QB70 .A53 2004
520'.74—dc22
                                    2003016156

We're going on a field trip to a planetarium.
We can't wait!

Things to find out:

How does a planetarium work?

What is a star made of?

Where do the stars go during the day?

Why is the moon different shapes
on different nights?

Welcome! I'm Mr. Solomon, the director of Star City Planetarium. You'll be my space detectives today. You can help me search for objects in the sky.

A planetarium has a theater with a big round ceiling, or dome. We'll go into the theater and turn out the lights. A special projector in the middle of the room will make the dome look like the night sky.

Let's go in now and find seats!

EXIT

INFO

PLANETARIUM

There are thousands of holes in a planetarium projector. These holes let light shine through to make dots of light on the ceiling. The dots look like stars, planets, and other space objects.

Some planetariums also use sound equipment, slide and video projectors, lasers, or computers to create a sky show.

5

Let's look up as the room darkens and watch the stars come out.
In the night sky, stars look like tiny dots of light, but they only
seem small because they are very far away.

Stars might look small, but they can be very large. They can be the size of Earth or even bigger than the sun. That's huge, because about one million Earths could fit inside the sun!

Stars are balls of gas that give off great heat and light. They shine all the time. You just can't see them during the day because the sun is so bright. Did you know that our sun is a star, too? It is the star closest to Earth. We couldn't live without the light and heat the sun gives us.

Earth is a big ball that spins in space. When our side of Earth faces the sun, we have daytime. When Earth turns, it becomes night for us and daytime for people on the other side of the world. Just like the other stars, the sun is always shining, even when we can't see it.

Look, space detectives. Can you tell what new object has appeared in our sky? Yes, it's the moon. The moon is Earth's nearest neighbor in space. It moves around Earth. The moon shines, but not with its own light, because the moon is made of rock. The moonlight we see is really the sun's light bouncing off the moon's surface.

 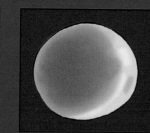 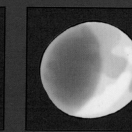 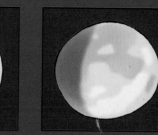 

New Moon   **Crescent Moon**   **Quarter Moon**   **Gibbous Moon**   **Full Moon**

Watch the moon every night and see how it changes. Sometimes it looks like a silver coin and sometimes like a pale banana. The moon doesn't really change shape, though. It is a ball, and the sun always lights up half of it. As the moon moves around Earth, we see different parts of the lit half of the moon. The shapes we see are called the phases of the moon.

Now, space detectives, be on the lookout for some points of light that are brighter than most stars. These may be planets. Like our moon, planets can't shine by themselves. They reflect the sun's light. Nine planets go around the sun in paths called orbits. Mercury is the planet closest to the sun, and Pluto is usually farthest away. The planets aren't nearly as close together as they appear here.

MERCURY

VENUS

EARTH

MARS

URANUS

PLUTO

SATURN

NEPTUNE

JUPITER

Let's look at the stars again. At first, all those dots of light might look the same and seem to be scattered every which way. But keep looking! You'll see that some stars are brighter than others, and you might notice patterns. People have imagined that these patterns look like certain people or animals. We call these star patterns constellations. So far, people have named 88 constellations. Look at the constellation we call Orion, the hunter in the sky. He is outlined here so you can see him more clearly. These outlines don't really appear in the sky!

Several of the stars in Orion are quite bright. Three of these stars make up Orion's belt. Sometimes you can see the stars that form the sword hanging from his belt.

Most constellations can be seen only during certain seasons, but a few can be seen every night. Look for the seven stars of the Big Dipper. Nearby, you might be able to spot the seven stars of the Little Dipper.

Follow a straight line from the front of the Big Dipper's cup to find the bright star at the end of the Little Dipper's handle. This star is called either Polaris or the North Star, because it is almost directly above Earth's North Pole. It has helped travelers find their way for centuries. When you face the North Star, you're facing north.

The solar system is what we call the sun and all the objects that travel around it, such as the planets with their moons. Solar means having to do with the sun. Our solar system is part of a huge group of stars and other space objects called a galaxy. The name of our galaxy is the Milky Way.

There are billions of stars in a galaxy and billions of galaxies. It's hard to imagine how big space is! We call all the galaxies put together the universe. The universe is *everything*, including Earth. We know about only a small part of the universe, but scientists are always trying to learn more.

I hope you've enjoyed the show and had fun being space detectives! Keep in mind that some scientists actually *are* space detectives. These scientists are called astronomers. They explore the mysteries of the universe. Some of you may become astronomers and be *real* space detectives one day.

Thanks for visiting Star City Planetarium. Come back for a sky show anytime! Look at the sky tonight, and see what you can find on your own.

IS A FULL MOON BIGGER WHEN IT'S LOW IN THE SKY?

What you need:

a full moon
1 dime

What you do:

1. Look at the full moon as it is rising and near the horizon, soon after the sky turns dark. (Many calendars show when there will be a full moon. There is usually one full moon each month.)

2. Now turn your back to the moon, bend over at your waist, and look at the moon upside down through your legs. Does the moon look the same size as it did when you were right-side up?

3. Stand up again, and look at the moon as you did in step 1. Stretch out your arm, and hold a dime up next to the moon. Notice how big the moon is compared to the dime.

4. Later in the night, when the moon is higher in the sky, compare the moon to the dime again. Is it the same size as it was in step 3?

A full moon is always the same size, but your eyes can play tricks on you. This is called the "moon illusion." Looking upside down changes the way you see the moon, so your eyes are no longer fooled. When you compare the moon with the dime, you prove that the moon is always the same size, no matter where it is in the sky.

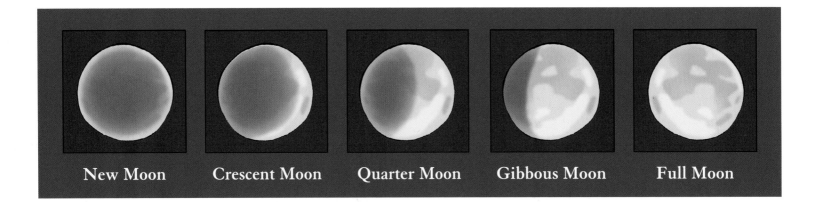

New Moon   Crescent Moon   Quarter Moon   Gibbous Moon   Full Moon

FUN FACTS

- A planetarium can show how the night sky looked at some time in the past, and it can show present or future night skies. It also can show how the night sky looks on the other side of the world.

- Our Milky Way galaxy has about as many stars as there are grains of sand in a sandbox—billions!

- If you look very closely, or with a telescope, you might see that stars are different colors. The hottest stars are blue or white. The coolest stars are red or orange. Stars with temperatures somewhere in between, like our sun, are yellow.

- One way to remember the usual order of the planets going out from the sun is to make up a sentence such as, "Many very early mornings Jack skated upon Ned's pond." The first letter of each word is the first letter of a planet's name, starting with Mercury, the planet closest to the sun. Can you name them all?

- The planets Mercury, Earth, Venus, and Mars are made mostly of rock with iron centers. Jupiter, Saturn, Uranus, and Neptune are mostly gas with small rock and iron centers. Scientists aren't sure what Pluto is made of.

- Most of the time, Pluto is the planet farthest from the sun, but Pluto's orbit is an unusual shape. Every 228 years, Pluto is closer to the sun than Neptune for 20 years. The last time this happened was from 1979 to 1999.

- Scientists are always making new discoveries. Some astronomers now think that Pluto may not be a planet at all! More information is needed to solve the mystery of Pluto. Stay tuned to see what space detectives discover next.

GLOSSARY

astronomer—a scientist who studies stars, planets, and other objects in space

constellation—a group of stars that seem to form a pattern or picture

galaxy—a large group of billions of stars, planets, and other matter such as dust and gas

orbit—the oval-shaped path one object takes around another object in space

planet—a large, ball-shaped object that travels around a star such as our sun and does not make its own light

planetarium—a building or room that has special equipment for projecting pictures of the stars, planets, and other space objects and their movements onto a rounded ceiling, or dome

reflect—to stop something and send it back or away. The moon and the planets reflect the sun's light.

solar system—our sun and all the objects that travel around the sun, such as the nine planets and their moons

star—a huge ball of gas that gives off heat and light

telescope—an instrument that makes faraway objects look larger and closer

universe—space and everything that exists within it, including Earth

TO LEARN MORE

At the Library

Bredeson, Carmen. *The Moon*. New York: Children's Press, 2003.

Croswell, Ken. *See the Stars: Your First Guide to the Night Sky*. Honesdale, Penn.: Boyds Mills Press, 2000.

Rau, Dana Meachen. *The Solar System*. Minneapolis: Compass Point Books, 2001.

Tomecek, Steve. *Stars*. Washington, D.C.: National Geographic, 2003.

Vogt, Gregory L. *The Milky Way*. Mankato, Minn.: Bridgestone Books, 2003.

On the Web

Fact Hound offers a safe, fun way to find Web sites related to this book. All of the sites on Fact Hound have been researched by our staff.
http://www.facthound.com

1. Visit the Fact Hound home page.
2. Enter a search word related to this book, or type in this special code: 1404802991.
3. Click on the FETCH IT button.

Your trusty Fact Hound will fetch the best sites for you!

INDEX